STEP INTO THE WORLD OF

ANCIENT

INDIA

CONTENTS

CONTENTS

HARAPPANS & ARYANS

Ancient Indian civilisation had many distinct phases – the Indus valley or Harappan civilisation, the Aryan civilisation and the Age of Empires.

An Urban Civilisation

The Indus Valley civilisation is the oldest. It existed at the same time as the Egyptian and Sumerian civilisations. Spread over Pakistan and Western India, it is also the world's largest ancient urban civilisation. The first cities of Harappa and Mohenjo Daro were discovered in the 1920s. Ever since then, archaeologists have been unearthing new and incredible facts about life 5000 years ago!

Arrival of the Aryans

The Indus Valley civilisation was followed by the Aryan civilisation. This era is divided into the Vedic and Epic periods. The four Vedas or religious texts were composed in the Vedic period. Today these texts tell us about Aryan lifestyles, customs and beliefs. The later Epic period saw the writing of the two greatest epics of India – *Mahabharata* and *Ramayana*.

In ancient India texts were written on palm leaves

HARAPPANS & ARYANS

 How many Indus Valley sites have been unearthed?

Archaeologists have discovered around 1400 Indus Valley sites to date. This civilisation was spread over 1.5 million km²! Apart from Harappa and Mohenjo-daro, other main cities are Rakhigarhi, Dholavira and the port of Lothal in India, and Ganeriwala in Pakistan.

 Were the Harappans ruled by kings?

It is not very clear whether they were ruled by kings. The discovery of the idol of a priest, however, has led to the belief that they were probably ruled by a "priest king".

 Were the Harappans skilled at town planning?

The discovery of Mohenjo-daro proved that the Harappans had amazing engineering skills. The city had well-planned streets and buildings similar to modern cities! It was divided into a citadel and a lower city. Streets were straight and had an advanced drainage system.

 Why is the Indus Valley civilisation also called the Harappan civilisation?

Harappa was the first Indus Valley city to be discovered. Situated near the Pakistani city of Lahore, archaeologists unearthed this city around 1921. That is why the Indus Valley civilisation is also known as the Harappan civilisation and the people of this civilisation called Harappans.

 Did the Aryans drive the Harappans away?

Until recently it was believed that the Aryans were responsible for wiping out the Harappan civilisation. But new studies show that the Harappans left their cities because of poor rainfall and a gradual drying up of trade with other civilisations.

 What is an excavation?

Archaeological excavations involve the discovery, recording and recovery of ancient materials that have remained buried for years. An excavation begins with locating the site by scientific methods. Sometimes an accidental discovery of ancient artefacts may lead to excavations too.

The idol of the Priest King

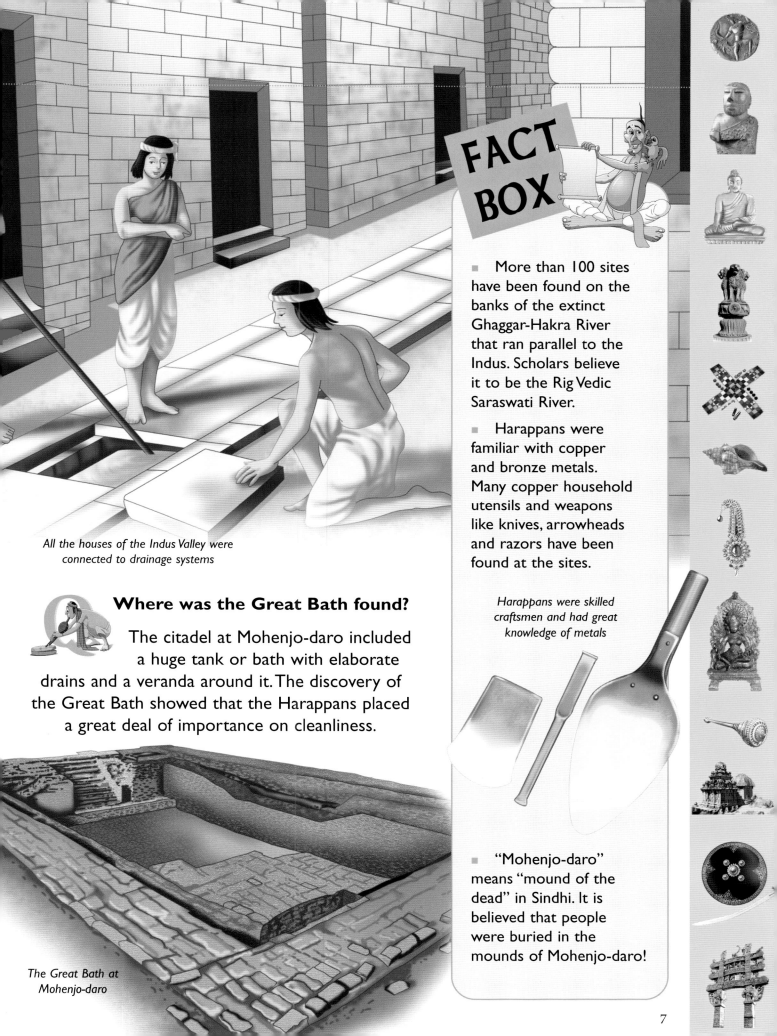

All the houses of the Indus Valley were connected to drainage systems

■ More than 100 sites have been found on the banks of the extinct Ghaggar-Hakra River that ran parallel to the Indus. Scholars believe it to be the Rig Vedic Saraswati River.

■ Harappans were familiar with copper and bronze metals. Many copper household utensils and weapons like knives, arrowheads and razors have been found at the sites.

Harappans were skilled craftsmen and had great knowledge of metals

Where was the Great Bath found?

The citadel at Mohenjo-daro included a huge tank or bath with elaborate drains and a veranda around it. The discovery of the Great Bath showed that the Harappans placed a great deal of importance on cleanliness.

■ "Mohenjo-daro" means "mound of the dead" in Sindhi. It is believed that people were buried in the mounds of Mohenjo-daro!

The Great Bath at Mohenjo-daro

HARAPPANS & ARYANS

Which are the four *Vedas*?

The four Vedas are the Rig Veda, Yajur Veda, Sama Veda and Atharva Veda. The Rig Veda – the first to be composed – has 10,552 verses!

A Brahmana priest

A Kshatriya warrior

What does the word *Veda* mean?

"Veda" means "knowledge". The Vedas were a collection of Sanskrit poems. For thousands of years they were orally passed down from one generation to the next. They were written down only towards the end of the 3rd century B.C.

Were the Aryans ruled by kings?

The Aryans had several tribes or ganas (group or clan). Each gana had a chief who led the tribe and made important decisions.

Who were the Aryans?

The Aryans were nomads from Central Asia who settled in northwest India around 1500 B.C.

What is the caste system?

Based on occupation, the Aryans were divided into four varnas or castes: Brahmanas, Kshatriyas, Vaishyas and Shudras. The Brahmanas were the learned priests while the Kshatriyas were rulers and warriors. The Vaishyas were farmers, craftsmen, traders and merchants and the Shudras were labourers.

EMIPRES OF ANCIENT INDIA

The Age of Empires began with the Mauryan dynasty in 321 B.C. Before that the country was divided into several small kingdoms, who constantly fought each other. This situation encouraged foreign conquerors like Alexander the Great to invade India.

The Mauryan Empire

Alexander managed to conquer a large part of Northwest India before he was forced by his tired soldiers to abandon his mission. After Alexander's death, Chandragupta Maurya defeated his heir, Seleacus Nicator and captured the region. He also defeated the powerful Nanda King of Magadha, Dhanananda and set up the Mauryan dynasty – the first empire of India.

The Chola Dynasty

Though the Mauryan dynasty extended its control over all of North India, the southern part of the country was firmly in the grasp of smaller kingdoms. The greatest of them all was the Chola dynasty. Trade with China flourished during this time, while art and architecture reached its peak.

Alexander the Great invaded India in 326 B.C.

Who was Bindusara?

Chandragupta Maurya was succeeded by his son Bindusara. The Mauryan Empire expanded vastly during his rule. Bindusara captured most of India except for Kalinga and the far south.

The famous Sanskrit poet Kalidasa lived during King Vikramaditya's reign

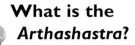

What is the *Arthashastra*?

The *Arthashastra* is a great political work. Written by Chandragupta Maurya's able minister, Chanakya or Kautilya, it deals with the duties of a government, maintenance of law and order, economics and the art of war. This ancient text continues to be relevant even to this day!

Chanakya was responsible for the establishment of the Mauryan Empire

Did Chandragupta Maurya meet Alexander?

Greek biographies of Alexander talk of a young man named Sandracottus, who urged Alexander to attack Magadha. This young man was perhaps Chandragupta Maurya.

Who was the greatest Mauryan emperor?

Ashoka the Great was the most famous Mauryan emperor. He was the grandson of Chandragupta Maurya and succeeded his father, Bindusara in around 272 B.C.

What happened after the death of Ashoka?

Ashoka's death marked the end of the Mauryan Empire. It broke up into smaller kingdoms. Brihadratha, the last Mauryan king, was killed by his own general, Pushyamitra Shunga. Once again the land was invaded by foreigners.

The pillar of Emperor Ashoka is now a symbol of the Indian Government

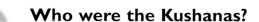

Who were the Kushanas?

The Kushanas were a nomadic tribe from China who invaded India after the fall of the Mauryan dynasty. They ruled a large part of North India and Afghanistan. Kanishka was the greatest Kushana ruler.

Which is the Golden Age of Indian culture?

Chandragupta Vikramaditya's reign is the Golden Age of Indian culture. Music, art and literature flourished in this era. Most of the Ajanta paintings and several famous Sanskrit works are from this age.

FACT BOX

■ In around 480 A.D., the Huns from China invaded India and defeated the Guptas. At first they conquered northern India and eventually expanded their control to the western region too.

■ The famous Bragatheeshwarar temple in Tanjore, dedicated to Lord Shiva was built by the great Chola king Rajaraja Cholan. The temple was named Rajarajeshwaram in his honour.

■ The kings of ancient India wore elaborate and rich costumes. They were also very fond of jewellery made of gold and precious stones. Apart from the crown, the Indian kings wore necklaces, bangles (*kadas*) and even earrings!

A turban pin worn by ancient Indian kings

When was the Gupta Empire established?

The Guptas were chieftains who ruled a small Magadha kingdom. But fortunes changed when the third king, Chandragupta I, got married to Lichchhavi princess Kumaradevi and received Pataliputra in dowry. Encouraged by his new status, Chandragupta built a small kingdom that marked the beginning of the Gupta Dynasty with Chandragupta as the first Gupta emperor.

An ancient gold coin from the Gupta period. These coins were called "dinaras"

What was King Harshavardhana famous for?

King Harshavardhana was not only a great conqueror but also a good administrator. He worked hard for his people. A huge part of the taxes were given away to the poor and needy!

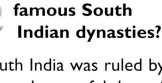

Which were the famous South Indian dynasties?

South India was ruled by several powerful dynasties like the Pallavas, Pandyas, Cholas and Cheras.

How did the Cholas become powerful?

Around 850 A.D., the Chola ruler Vijayalaya defeated the Pallavas and captured Tanjore. The Cholas then extended their power to a large part of South India. They reached their peak under the rule of Rajaraja Cholan and his son, Rajendra Cholan.

A statue of the great Chola king Rajaraja Cholan

Which Chinese traveller visited India during Chandragupta Vikramaditya's rule?

Fa Hien, a Chinese Pilgrim, spent 11 years in India – travelling and studying Sanskrit. We know all about Vikramaditya's rule from his writings.

WARS & WEAPONS

Excavations at the Indus Valley sites suggest that Harappans were a peace loving people. Though the cities were protected against invasions, there is little evidence of any great source of violence. But wars became common after the Aryans arrived. Aryan literature shows that they placed a lot of importance on wars and maintained large armies. That is how the *Kshatriya* warrior class was formed. Only *Kshatriyas* were trained and allowed to fight and as a rule a non-*Kshatriya* could not become a king. There were many laws of war – for example, it was unlawful to attack an unarmed person.

Of Swords and Shields

Ancient Indians were well trained in the art of various weapons. It was compulsory for all warriors to know sword fighting and archery. Horses and elephants formed an important part of the army. They were also brilliant at military strategies and a lot of their formations were based on the game of *chaturanga* or chess.

Swords and shields were among the chief weapons of ancient India

WARS & WEAPONS

Why did Ashoka give up war?

In an attempt to expand his kingdom, Ashoka attacked Kalinga. Thousands of people were killed in this terrible battle (260 B.C.). Ashoka was deeply shaken by the destruction he had caused. He vowed never to fight again and converted to Buddhism!

Kalingaraj Emperor Ashoka during the Kalinga War

What is the *Chaturangabala*?

The *Chaturangabala* was a popular battle formation used by ancient Indians. It was named after the game, *Chaturanga* and consisted of the infantry (foot soldiers) followed by rows of horses, elephants and chariots.

What other battle formations did they use?

The ancient Indians used another formation called the *Sadanga* or the six-fold army. Apart from the four common forces, the *Sadanga* also included the commissariat and the navy. The commissariat carried medical supplies, physicians and additional weapons.

A warrior's armour

Did they wear armour during wars?

Apart from *dhoti*, warriors wore armoured vests and camel skin shoes. They also wore helmets, amulets and good luck charms. According to the *Arthashastra*, soldiers used powders from fireflies and wild boars's eyes to see better at night!

Were firearms used?

The *Vedas* and epics contain descriptions of weapons called the "*agni astra*", meaning firearms and the use of explosives like the *viswasaghati* that burst on contact! There are also descriptions for rockets suggesting that warfare in ancient India was highly advanced.

How were weapons classified?

Weapons in ancient India were classified into three main groups. The *mukta* (thrown), the *amukta* (not thrown) and the *mantramukta* (discharged by mantras). The bow and arrow fell under the first category, while *amukta* weapons included battle-axes and swords.

Kings and generals rode on chariots

Who fought the Battle of Jhelum?

The Battle of Jhelum, also called the Battle of Hydaspes, was fought between Alexander and Porus – an Indian king who refused to surrender to the Greeks. Porus fought valiantly till he was captured. Impressed, Alexander freed Porus and returned his kingdom!

FACT BOX

■ The *Urumi* is a lethal weapon used by *Kalaripayattu* warriors. It is a six-foot-long flexible sword, usually worn around the waist.

■ Ancient Indians used a very unusual group of spies called *Vishakanyas* or "poison-maidens"! These women were fed small doses of poison that was transmitted to the victim – usually kings. They also poisoned the king's food after gaining his affections.

■ The mace or the *gada* was an important weapon. It was a heavy rod with spikes on top. It is said that the mace could break rocks and even kill elephants!

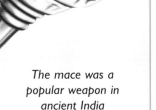

The mace was a popular weapon in ancient India

WARS & WEAPONS

Did any martial art exist in ancient India?

Kalaripayattu is widely regarded as the oldest form of martial art. It probably gave rise to *Kung-fu*. According to a story, Boddhi Dharma – the father of Zen Buddhism – trained Shaolin monks in *Kalaripayattu* to help them defend themselves against bandits!

Kalaripayattu warriors in action

Was naval warfare known?

Ancient Indians had extremely organised naval fleets. Chandragupta Maurya even had a naval department in his government, headed by a *Nauvadhyaksha* or superintendent.

Were spies used?

Ancient India had perfected the art of espionage! Chanakya's *Arthashastra* contains detailed descriptions of spies and their methods. The Indian secret service still follows Chanakya's recommendations.

How did spies operate?

Spies disguised themselves as holy men, beggars, artists or merchants and collected information from the enemy state. They also spread false reports and caused confusion among the enemy. Double agents were also popular!

What are the origins of *Kalaripayattu*?

Kalaripayattu originated in the South Indian state of Kerala. Legends trace it back to Lord Parasurama, the creator of Kerala. But history says *it* evolved into a martial art during the rule of the Cheras. They adopted it for fighting the Cholas and Pandyas.

A Kshatriya prince being trained in archery

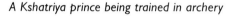

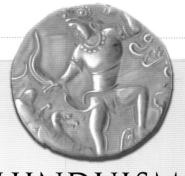

HINDUISM

India is a land of many religions. The majority of Indians follow Hinduism – the world's oldest living religion. It is believed that it existed even before the arrival of the Aryans. But Hinduism, as we know it today, evolved after the Aryans settled in India. It spread widely during the Vedic and the Epic periods.

Gods & Goddesses

In the beginning, ancient Indians (Harappans) worshipped the forces of nature. The sun, rivers, mountains, seas and oceans were the main deities. This was later followed by a belief in one God. The various gods and goddesses were in fact the *avatars* (incarnations or different forms) of this one God. The most important Hindu gods are Brahma, Vishnu and Shiva. Called the *Trimurti*, this trinity represents birth, existence and death. Brahma is the creator, Vishnu the preserver and Shiva is the destroyer of the Universe!

The Trimurti represented the Supreme God

HINDUISM

Who is the God of Knowledge?

Lord Ganesha is the Hindu God of Knowledge. He is also the remover of obstacles. His blessings are always sought at the beginning of all auspicious occasions like, weddings, moving house and beginning education.

What are the *Pancha Mahabhoota*?

The *Pancha Mahabhoota* are the five sacred forces of nature: earth, fire, water, air and sky. Fire and water are used in religious rituals even today. Water from the sacred River Ganga is given to the dying, cleansing them of all sins and ensuring a berth in heaven!

Lord Ganesha is one of the most popular Hindu Gods

What objects are symbols of holiness?

Coconuts are believed to be God's fruit! They are offered at temples or during pujas (prayer) along with flowers and incense sticks. Mango and betel leaves, banana saplings and areca nuts are also sacred.

What is reincarnation?

According to Hinduism, all creatures go through an endless cycle of birth and death. A person may be reborn as an animal or plant in his next life, and vice-versa! This is reincarnation.

Why do Hindus perform *Suryanamaskara*?

The Sun is the giver of life and the observer of the Universe. Hindus believe that performing the *Suryanamaskara* (Sun-worshipping ritual) will cure them of all diseases, wipe away their sins and bring them prosperity and happiness!

A Hindu Brahmana offering morning prayers, or Suryanamaskara, at the holy River Ganga

Meditation is now an integral part of Yoga

FACT BOX

■ *Moksha* releases a person from the eternal cycle of birth and death. When a person continues to perform all duties with sincerity throughout his different lifetimes, his soul attains *Moksha* and is never reborn again!

■ Lord Vishnu is yet to appear as Kalki, his tenth incarnation! It is said that Kalki will come to rescue us when evil on earth reaches an unbearable level.

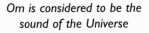

Om is considered to be the sound of the Universe

■ The word "Amen" has perhaps come from *Omkar* or *Om* – representing the Universe. It is also spelt "AUM" and stands for the *Trimurti* in Hinduism. These three letters also symbolise heaven, earth and hell!

What is the importance of meditation?

Ancient sages meditated to achieve the goal of becoming one with God. Meditation requires a person to give up all comforts and concentrate totally on this goal. Sages underwent rigorous methods and would even abstain from eating for weeks at a time!

What traditional rituals were performed before entering a temple?

Ancient Indians never entered a temple without taking a bath. This was believed to purify a person physically and spiritually. All Hindu pilgrimages were on riverbanks and temples had ponds near them. Devotees also removed their shoes outside the temple as a show of respect for God.

19

HINDUISM

Which are the most popular Hindu deities?

The lords Shiva, Krishna, Rama, Hanuman (the monkey God) and the goddesses Durga, Kali, Lakshmi and Saraswati are commonly worshipped by Hindus. They also worship the nine planet deities known as Navagraha. These grahas or planets are said to have a great impact on a person's life to cure diseases and predict the future!

Did Hindu deities have special modes of transport?

Most Hindu deities are believed to possess transport in the form of birds or animals. Shiva travels on a white bull named Nandi, while Goddess Durga uses a lion. Lord Vishnu's vehicle is the eagle and Lord Karthikeya, the God of War, flies around on a peacock! Interestingly, the elephant God, Ganesha's, mode of transport is a tiny mouse!

What does the word *Karma* mean?

Hinduism believes that man is ultimately responsible for his happiness and sufferings, not God. He is rewarded or punished according to his karma or deeds. Our karma could bring us results in this life as well as in a later life!

Why is a *Yagna* conducted?

A *Yagna* is a sacrifice made to Agni, the God of fire. It is performed for prosperity and well being. During this ritual a fire is lit in a special fireplace, sacred mantras are chanted and grains, *ghee* (clarified butter), sandalwood and other ingredients are used.

Priests performing a Yagna or a fire-sacrifice ritual

How many *avatars* or incarnations does Lord Vishnu have?

The *Dasavatara* or ten incarnations of Lord Vishnu are as *Matsya* (the fish), *Kurma* (the tortoise), *Varaha* (the boar), *Narasimha* (the half-man, half-lion), *Vamana* (the dwarf), *Parasurama* (the warrior sage), *Rama* (the ideal king), *Krishna* (the cowherd), *Buddha* (the enlightened one) and *Kalki* (the horse rider). Interestingly, all these *avatars* are mortals while Vishnu is indestructible and lives forever!

BUDDHISM & JAINISM

India is also the birthplace of Buddhism and Jainism. Both these religions were born as movements against the strict rituals of Hinduism during the Vedic period. Their birth also marked the beginning of secularism in India, wherein people of various religions co-existed. The stories of the two founders – Gautama Buddha and Mahavira – are very similar. The basic principles of both religions include *ahimsa* (non-violence) and respect for all living beings.

The Story of a Prince
Gautama Buddha (Siddhartha) was the son of King Shudhodhana and Queen Maya. Acting upon the advice of a sage, the king kept his son away from all sufferings. The prince grew up knowing only riches and happiness. He knew nothing about sickness or death, until one day, when he accidentally witnessed the sufferings of his people. Shocked by this knowledge, Siddhartha left his royal life in search of a solution to human misery.

Lord Buddha, the Enlightened One

What did King Bimbisara offer Gautama Buddha?

When Gautama arrived at Rajagriha, the capital of Magadha, King Bimbisara went to meet him. Impressed, the king offered him a part of his kingdom. But Gautama turned down the offer saying that he was in search of enlightenment.

King Bimbisara offering a part of his kingdom to Buddha

What is the significance of yellow in Buddhism?

Buddhist monks in ancient India wore yellow robes. The colour is said to represent the earth. Yellow also stood for autumn leaves symbolising the Buddhist philosophy that everything has to wither and die someday.

Who were *Bhikkhus*?

Buddhist monks were known as *Bhikkhus* (mendicants). They lived a very strict life. The only things they owned were a begging bowl, a walking stick and a pair of sandals!

Buddhist monks could receive alms only if given willingly

Did the Buddha perform any miracles?

According to legend, a woman once asked the Buddha to bring her dead son back to life. Instead of working a miracle, she was asked to bring three mustard seeds from a family where no one had died. The woman went from door to door, only to be told that there had been at least one death in each family. The truth slowly dawned on the woman, who later became the Buddha's disciple.

Why did Buddhism split?

The *Mahayana* group of Buddhists gave up the rigorous lives of earlier monks and accepted Buddha as their God. Idol worship was practised and rituals were borrowed from Hinduism. They also preferred Sanskrit to the original Pali scriptures. The *Hinayanas* continued to follow the original path of the Buddha.

Did Buddhists believe in prayers?

Originally, Buddhism did not have any God or Devil. It preached that desire was the cause of all sufferings. Hence happiness could be found by giving up desire – not by praying!

How did Emperor Ashoka popularise Buddhism?

Buddhism became a state religion during Emperor Ashoka's reign. He sent missionaries not only all over India, but also to Sri Lanka, West Asia, Central Asia and China. He also built several stupas with Buddhist inscriptions on them.

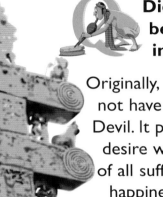

The gateway to the famous Stupa at Sanchi

FACT BOX

■ The Buddha attained enlightenment while he sat meditating under a fig tree. It was called the *Mahabodhi* tree, meaning the tree of revelation.

■ Jain monks have to carry a broom to sweep the path before them – for keeping all living organisms from harm!

■ Buddhism is represented by eight auspicious symbols. The umbrella, the golden fish, the treasure vase, the lotus, the conch, the auspicious knot, the victory banner and the Dharma-wheel.

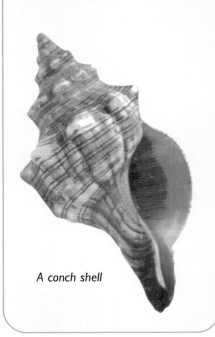

A conch shell

BUDDHISM & JAINISM

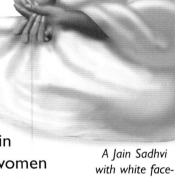

A Jain Sadhvi with white face-cloth and sari

Who was Bahubali?

Bahubali was the elder son of a king named Rishabha. Legend tells that Bahubali gave up his kingdom and went to the forest to meditate. It is said that this Jain sage stood naked and did not eat for a year. He remained so still and silent that vines and creepers grew up his body!

The famous Bahubali statue at Shravana-belgola is 58 feet tall

Who are Sadhvis?

Unlike Buddhists, who did not readily welcome women into their fold in the ancient days, the *Swetambar* group of Jains allowed women to join their order. These women saints were called *Sadhvis*.

What are the two sects of Jainism?

Jain monks fall into two groups – the *Digambars* and the *Swetambars*. The *Digambars* are the older and stricter sect. They do not wear clothes and believe that women cannot become saints unless they are reborn as men. The *Swetambars* wear an unstitched white cloth and allow women into their sect.

Why do Jain monks wear masks?

Jain monks never bathed for fear of unknowingly destroying some living being! For the same reason, they travel only on foot and cover their mouth with a piece of white cloth to prevent killing organisms in the air while breathing!

Who is Bodhisattva Maitreya?

Like the Hindus, the Buddhists also believe that when earth becomes burdened with evil, Buddha will reappear to restore *dhamma* (order and religion). The Bodhisattva Maitreya represents this incarnation of the Buddha.

DAILY LIFE

Life in ancient India was very advanced from the time of the Harappan civilisation. They were architectural geniuses, who built amazing towns and houses. Their main occupation was agriculture. The Harappans were also skilled potters and metal workers. Ancient India had excellent trade relations with Mesopotamia, Greece, Rome and China. They ate simple food. Aryans ate both vegetarian and non-vegetarian food. But following the spread of Buddhism and Jainism, most of the population became vegetarians.

A Shudra with his broom and basket. In ancient india, Shudras were given the responsibility of maintaining civic cleanliness

Caste & Clothes

Ancient Indians mostly wore cotton. Cotton formed a large part of their cultivation. Their simple clothes also helped to identify their caste. The *Brahmanas* wore white while the *Kshatriyas* preferred red and the *Vaishyas* yellow. Ancient Indians were also very fond of jewellery. Both men and women wore elaborate jewellery skillfully crafted out of copper, gold and precious stones. Royalty and noblemen adorned themselves with rich silks and gold.

DAILY LIFE

What is known about ancient Indian coins?

The earliest known coins were minted in central India around the fifth century B.C. The first coins were made of silver and had punch marks. Later, gold coins were also introduced.

Did the Aryans build houses too?

The Aryans were a nomadic tribe. They settled down after coming to India. Houses during the Vedic period were made of mud or wood with thatched roofs. Royal palaces during the Age of Empires were also made of wood.

Did ancient Indians use boats and ships?

Seals with pictures of boats dug up from the Indus Valley sites show that ancient Indians used flat-bottomed boats with sails. These were mainly used for trade. Later, during the Age of Empires, ships and boats were used in wars.

Where did the Harappans store their grains?

During excavations, archaeologists discovered a huge building resembling a storage facility. The Harappans probably used it for storing grains. Some believe that this "Granary" was perhaps also used for public meetings and religious gatherings.

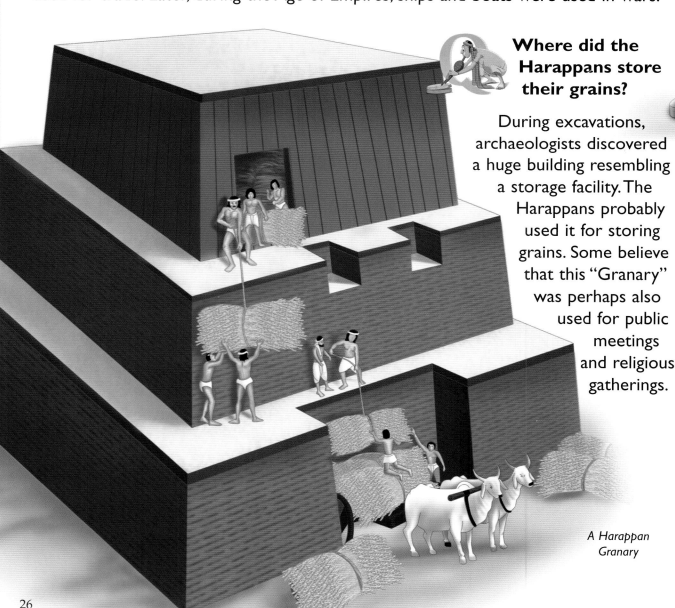

A Harappan Granary

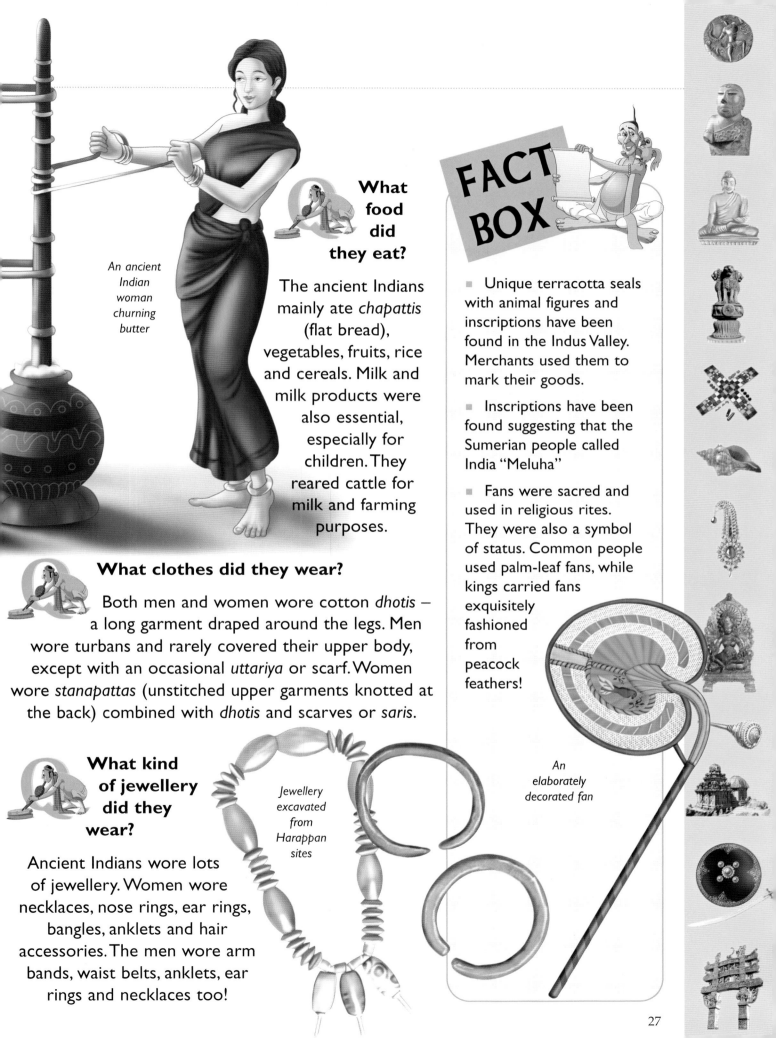

An ancient Indian woman churning butter

What food did they eat?

The ancient Indians mainly ate *chapattis* (flat bread), vegetables, fruits, rice and cereals. Milk and milk products were also essential, especially for children. They reared cattle for milk and farming purposes.

What clothes did they wear?

Both men and women wore cotton *dhotis* – a long garment draped around the legs. Men wore turbans and rarely covered their upper body, except with an occasional *uttariya* or scarf. Women wore *stanapattas* (unstitched upper garments knotted at the back) combined with *dhotis* and scarves or *saris*.

What kind of jewellery did they wear?

Ancient Indians wore lots of jewellery. Women wore necklaces, nose rings, ear rings, bangles, anklets and hair accessories. The men wore arm bands, waist belts, anklets, ear rings and necklaces too!

Jewellery excavated from Harappan sites

FACT BOX

- Unique terracotta seals with animal figures and inscriptions have been found in the Indus Valley. Merchants used them to mark their goods.

- Inscriptions have been found suggesting that the Sumerian people called India "Meluha"

- Fans were sacred and used in religious rites. They were also a symbol of status. Common people used palm-leaf fans, while kings carried fans exquisitely fashioned from peacock feathers!

An elaborately decorated fan

27

DAILY LIFE

What did ancient Indians export?

Inscriptions found from Sumerian sites indicate that they bought various kinds of beads, gold and ivory handicrafts from India. Exquisite jewellery made from semi-precious stones was also in great demand.

What kind of houses did the Harappans live in?

Harappans lived in identical houses. They were built of baked brick and had flat roofs. All houses opened into a central courtyard and were connected to an advanced drainage system. Every house had a private bathroom and wells.

Ancient Indians extensively used the waterways for trade and transportation

Did ancient Indians wear silk?

Cotton and wool were the most popular materials in the early days. Ancient Indians were not aware of silk until later. Though silk came to India from China, ancient Indians were familiar with the process of making silk and had started to produce their own.

What mode of transport did they use?

Bullock carts were the most common mode of transport in ancient India. Camels, elephants and horses were used for long journeys. The rich and their womenfolk travelled by palanquins.

An ancient artefact depicting palanquin-bearers

What was their main occupation?

Apart from farming, ancient Indians made beautiful pottery, sculptures and jewellery. They also built roads and other public facilities. Cattle rearing and making chariots and weapons were other popular occupations.

ART & ARCHITECTURE

The ancient Indians were talented artists and architects; they made magnificent temples and monuments. The Harappans were brilliant engineers too. Ancient Harappan cities are examples of their mastery of building techniques. They were also excellent artisans, who created beautiful pottery and sculptures. Indian art reached its peak during the Age of Empires. Each empire had its signature art form that reflected its life and times.

The Magic of Creation

Art and architecture in ancient India was deeply influenced by religious beliefs and social customs of the time. Most sculptures were of the various deities, but they also depicted scenes from the great epics. There was a great artistic shift during the Age of Empires, when Buddhism became the dominant influence. Several *stupas* were constructed and numerous paintings and sculptures of the life of the Buddha were created.

An ancient Indian artisan at work

Were they skilled at metal work?

Ancient Indians were aware of the technology of smelting and also of mixing two or more metals. Coins and bronze sculptures of the period prove that they used advanced technologies and had knowledge of chemical engineering too!

How did ancient Indians build temples?

Most ancient Indian temples had one thing in common – they were all decorated with elaborate sculptures. Interestingly, stone blocks were not fixed with mortar but were held together by the force of gravity!

What is unique about *Kalamkari*?

Kalamkari is an ancient Indian craft of textile printing that uses vegetable dyes. The word literally means "pen-work" ("kalam" meaning "pen" and "kari" meaning "work"). Only the four colours of black, red, yellow and blue are used! Traditionally, scenes from the epics, *Mahabharata* and *Ramayana* and other Hindu legends are used.

A Kalamkari artist first sharpens a bamboo stick

He then ties a piece of cloth around this stick and dips it in ink

The flow of ink is controlled by pressing the cloth

What is *Gandhara* art?

Gandhara art is named after its place of origin – Gandhara in Pakistan. It was used to depict some of the earliest images of the Buddha. This style was highly influenced by Greek art.

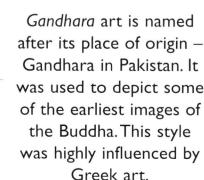

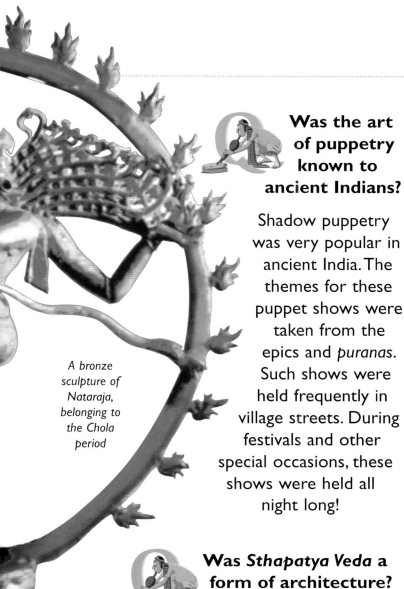

A bronze sculpture of Nataraja, belonging to the Chola period

Was the art of puppetry known to ancient Indians?

Shadow puppetry was very popular in ancient India. The themes for these puppet shows were taken from the epics and *puranas*. Such shows were held frequently in village streets. During festivals and other special occasions, these shows were held all night long!

Was *Sthapatya Veda* a form of architecture?

Sthapatya Veda is a part of *Atharva Veda* and deals with the science of architecture. The word, "sthapan" means "to build" and "veda" means "knowledge".

Was the Bamiyan Buddha in Afghanistan built by the ancient Indians?

Under King Kanishka, two huge statues of Buddha were carved from the cliffs of Bamiyan valley in Afghanistan. It was the first time that the Buddha was depicted as a man. Before that he was represented by symbols – like his footprints, an empty throne and the wheel of life. In 2001, the statues were destroyed by Taliban terrorists.

FACT BOX

- The Kailashnath temple at Ellora is the world's largest rock cut temple. It took over a hundred years to carve the temple out of a single rock!

- *Tholumattu* shadow puppets of South India were around five feet tall and were made from the hides of animals that died of natural causes!

- After coating wax figures with clay, ancient Indians melted the wax for clay moulds. They then filled the mould with molten metal. Once cooled, the clay mould was broken to reveal incredible metal figurines!

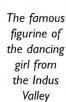

The famous figurine of the dancing girl from the Indus Valley

ART & ARCHITECTURE

What is *Vaastu Shastra*?

It is the science of building houses, temples and other structures. It mainly stresses the need for a balance between man and his natural surroundings. *Vaastu Shastra* combines science with art, astronomy and astrology.

According to *Vaastu Shastra*, how should one build a house?

Vaastu Shastra says that areas at the end of a road or close to graveyards should be avoided. Other elements like sources of water, trees and the size and shape of the land are to be taken into consideration.

A famous Ajanta cave painting

The magnificient temple architecture of Mahabalipuram

Why are the caves at Ajanta and Ellora special?

The Ajanta caves were Buddhist retreats and the monks carved out the beautiful figures using everyday tools! The structures at the Ellora caves represent Hinduism, Buddhism and Jainism.

Is the direction of a house important to *Vaastu Shastra*?

The placement of rooms and materials inside the house is more important than the direction it faces. For example, *Vaastu Shastra* says that money should be kept in cupboards placed in the south, facing north. This is because north is the direction of Kuber, the God of Wealth.

Why is Mahabalipuram famous?

Mahabalipuram, a port town of the Pallava dynasty, remains a magnificent example of Dravidian art and architecture. It is famous for its sandstone rock carvings and temples. The carving called, "Descent of the Ganges", is the world's largest open-air relief sculpture!

SCIENCE & LITERATURE

Ancient Indians made extraordinary contributions to the fields of science and literature. They made great advances in mathematics, medicine and astrology. They invented zero and gave the world the unique herbal therapy of Ayurveda. They were also the first to correctly calculate the circumference of the earth and to learn that the earth rotates on its own axis and moves around the sun. They also knew that the sun was, in fact, a star!

A famous scene from the Bhagavata Gita, a vital part of the epic Mahabharata

Vedas and Epics

Though we know that the Harappans could read and write, Indian literature truly developed from the Vedic period. The Hindu scriptures (*Vedas* and *Upanishads*) are the oldest known documents in the world. However, Indian literature reached its peak during the Gupta period. Many of the great works of Sanskrit literature belong to this period, which is rightly called the Golden Age of Indian culture.

SCIENCE & LITERATURE

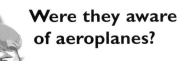

Were they aware of aeroplanes?

The *Vedas* and epics talk about various kinds of "flying machines" called *vimanas*. In the epic, *Ramayana*, Lord Rama returns to Ayodhya in a *Pushpaka Vimana* after defeating Ravana. Though there are no remains of such machines, archaeologists have found seals with pictures of "flying machines" from the Indus Valley sites that are similar to helicopters!

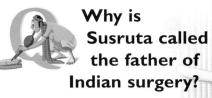

Why is Susruta called the father of Indian surgery?

Susruta was a great surgeon who served in the court of Chandragupta Vikramaditya. He wrote *Susruta Samhita*, an elaborate book on surgery. It is said that Susruta could even perform plastic surgery!

What does Varahamihira's *Pancha Siddhantika* contain?

Varahamihira was one of the *navaratnas* or nine gems of King Vikramaditya's court. He was a famous philosopher and mathematician, who wrote the valuable book on astronomy called *Pancha Siddhantika*. It contains details on how to calculate eclipses!

The ancient Ayurvedic physician, Susruta, performing surgery on a patient

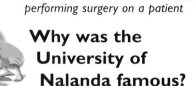

Why was the University of Nalanda famous?

Famous personalities like Aryabhatta and Chanakya studied in the University of Nalanda. It had around 10,000 students and over 1000 teachers! Though *Mahayana* Buddhism was the main subject, students were also taught grammar, astronomy and mathematics. Students from all over the world came here and were admitted on the basis of an entrance test.

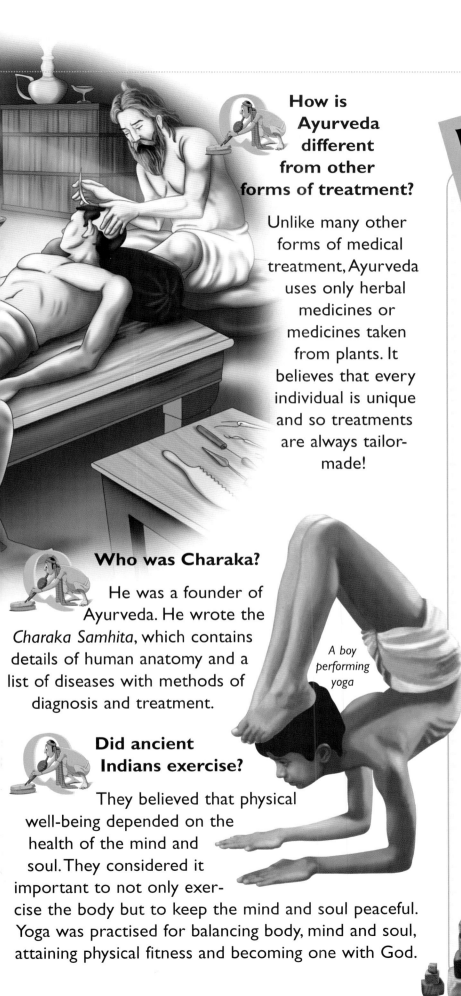

How is Ayurveda different from other forms of treatment?

Unlike many other forms of medical treatment, Ayurveda uses only herbal medicines or medicines taken from plants. It believes that every individual is unique and so treatments are always tailor-made!

Who was Charaka?

He was a founder of Ayurveda. He wrote the *Charaka Samhita*, which contains details of human anatomy and a list of diseases with methods of diagnosis and treatment.

Did ancient Indians exercise?

They believed that physical well-being depended on the health of the mind and soul. They considered it important to not only exercise the body but to keep the mind and soul peaceful. Yoga was practised for balancing body, mind and soul, attaining physical fitness and becoming one with God.

A boy performing yoga

FACT BOX

■ Dhanvantari is the God of Medicine. According to legend, he was born as the King of Kasi in order to end human sufferings from disease. He prepared documents on Ayurveda, which were passed on to his student, Susruta.

■ The world's first university was established in Taxila (Takshashila) around 700 B.C. It had over 10,000 students from all over the world studying more than 60 subjects!

■ The decimal system was developed by the mathematician, Pingala, around 100 B.C. The rules for using zero were introduced by Brahmagupta, who said that adding or subtracting any number with zero gave the same number. He also said that any number multiplied by zero would be zero!

Harappans followed an advanced weight-system

SCIENCE & LITERATURE

Did Harappans know how to read and write?

The Harappans had their own script. Various seals discovered at the Indus Valley sites prove this. But scientists have been unable to understand this script. The writings on the seals were short and simple, suggesting that the Harappans did not have a very complicated script.

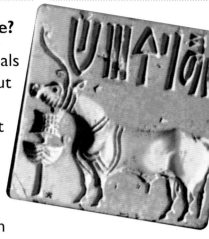

Did they know about algebra?

Algebra was born in ancient India around fifth century A.D. It was known as *Bijaganitam* ("bija" means "second" and "ganitam" means "mathematics"). Algebra was developed as a quicker system that was more effective for making astronomical calculations.

A Harappan seal with the ancient script that remains to be decoded

Who wrote *Abhijnanam Sakuntalam*?

The famous Sanskrit poet and playwright, Kalidasa, was a member of King Vikramaditya's court. He wrote many poems and plays that have become classics. His most famous works are *Abhijnanam Sakuntalam, Meghdootam, Raghuvamsham, Kumarasambhava* and *Malavikagnimitram.*

Aryabhatta, the ancient Indian astronomer, who was the first to talk about the earth's rotation

What system of education did they follow?

Ancient Indians followed the *gurukula* system of education. Children were sent to *ashrams* or schools, where they lived with their guru or teacher for about 12 years – learning the *Vedas* and *Upanishads*. Students were also taught Ayurveda, mathematics, music, astrology and even the art of self-defence and how to use weapons!

What was Aryabhatta's contribution to the field of science?

Aryabhatta was a great Indian astronomer and mathematician. He wrote the famous book on astronomy, *Aryabhatiya*. He was the first to say that the earth rotated on its own axis and revolved around the sun. He also explained that the sun was the source of moonlight too!

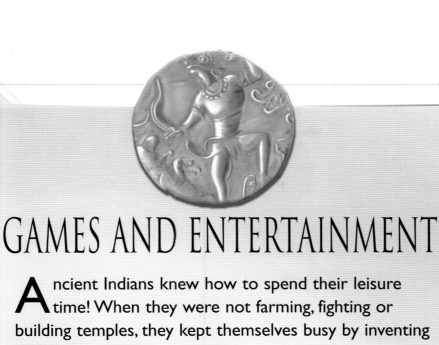

GAMES AND ENTERTAINMENT

Ancient Indians knew how to spend their leisure time! When they were not farming, fighting or building temples, they kept themselves busy by inventing games and learning the fine art of music and dance. They had many games – from the earliest form of chess (*chaturanga*) to playing cards and wrestling. Chariot-racing and hunting were extremely popular among the kings and noblemen.

A Musical History

Music was an integral part of life in ancient India. This can be understood from the fact that musical instruments like harps, drums, reed flutes and clay whistles were found in Harappa and Mohenjo-daro. The *Vedas* themselves were written in musical form and had to be chanted. Musical instruments accompanied the chants. The ancient Indians also found time for dance and theatre. They wrote plays and developed various classical dance forms that still exist in India.

An exquisitely crafted yazh or harp in the form of a peacock

GAMES AND ENTERTAINMENT

What is a *raga*?

A *raga* is the basic unit of Indian music. *Raga* or melody consists of seven different notes – the *sapta swaras*. They are *Sa* (*Sadjam*), *Ri* (*Rishabham*), *Ga* (*Gaandharam*), *Ma* (*Madhyamam*), *Pa* (*Pancham*), *Dha* (*Dhaivadam*) and *Ni* (*Nishadam*). They are similar to *Do, Re, Mi, Fa, So, La, Ti*!

How was the *Natya Shastra* written?

According to legend, the gods approached Lord Brahma, asking for recreation. Brahma took literature from the *Rig Veda*, songs from *Sama Veda*, expressions from *Yajur Veda* and emotions from *Atharva Veda* to compose the *Natya Veda*. He then related it to Bharata Muni who composed the *Natya Shastra*!

Were drums known to them?

The earliest drum, used by the Harappans, was the hour glass-shaped *hudukka*. Vedic singers used the *dundhubi*, which later evolved into drums like the *pushkara, mridangam, bhanda vadya* and *tabla*.

Indian dance and music reached its peak during the Gupta period

The chaturanga playing board, counters and dice

What kind of game was *pittu*?

Pittu is an ancient game, which continues to be popular amongst children. In this game, a number of flat stones are piled on top of each other. A child strikes down the stones with a ball and piles them up again for others to try.

How is *Chaturanga* different from chess?

Chaturanga was played by four players with coloured pieces and two dice. It was more a game of luck. Unlike chess, there was no bishop or queen, elephants and ministers were used instead.

38

Is Nataraja an *avatar* of Lord Shiva?

Lord Shiva is also known as Nataraja, the "King of Dancers". His cosmic dance represents creation, preservation and destruction. It also stands for the balance between good and evil and is called the "dance of life".

Was dance and music performed only in temples?

In ancient India, dance and music were largely dedicated to Gods and were performed in temples. Only a special group of dancers called *devadasis* performed these arts. "Devadasis", meaning "servants of god", were girls dedicated to temples for serving priests and taking part in daily rituals.

Is *Natya Shastra* the only ancient document available on performing arts?

An older document, the *Naradiyashiksha*, contains descriptions of *Vedic* and *Gandharva* music. Written around 100 B.C., this book defines *Gandharva* music on the basis of the three elements: *swara*, *taala* and *paada*.

FACT BOX

Playing cards from ancient India were made of cloth

■ In ancient India, a popular game of cards called *Kridapatram* ("playing leaves"), was played by the royalty and nobility. Apart from the common pack of 12 sets, there also existed packs of eight, nine and ten sets. These circular cards were painted with scenes from the *Ramayana* and *Mahabharata*.

■ King Harshavardhana wrote great Sanskrit plays like *Ratnavali, Priyadarshika* and *Nagananda*. After his reign, Sanskrit theatre declined due to the absence of royal support.

■ Saraswati, the Goddess of Learning, is depicted as holding a *veena*. The *veena* is an early stringed instrument that continues to play an important role in Indian classical music.

GAMES AND ENTERTAINMENT

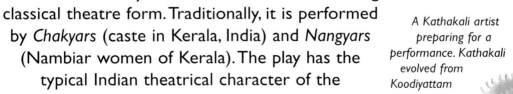

Hunting or "mrigaya" on elephant-back was a favourite royal sport

Did ancient Indians write plays?

The earliest known Sanskrit plays were written between the first and tenth century A.D. The two great epics – *Mahabharata* and *Ramayana* – have been the basis of several plays. Sanskrit theatre reached its peak during the Gupta period. Kalidasa, the greatest classical playwright, belonged to this period.

Did kings play games too?

Kings of ancient India indulged in competitions like chariot racing, sword fighting, wrestling and gambling. Hunting was also a favourite pastime.

A Kathakali artist preparing for a performance. Kathakali evolved from Koodiyattam

What is unusual about *Koodiyattam*?

Koodiyattam is the only surviving Sanskrit theatre form today and the world's oldest existing classical theatre form. Traditionally, it is performed by *Chakyars* (caste in Kerala, India) and *Nangyars* (Nambiar women of Kerala). The play has the typical Indian theatrical character of the *Vidhooshaka* or jester who acts as the narrator.

Is there any difference between *rasa* and *bhava*?

Rasa and *bhava* are the most important parts of any performance. *Bhava* is a particular state of mind, while the *rasa* is the expression of that emotion. There are nine *bhavas* and nine corresponding *rasas* (*navarasa*). They include love, anger, wonder, fear, humour, bravery and more.

DID YOU KNOW?

The beliefs and customs of ancient Indians were driven by their religion. Customs also differed regionally. The vastness of the country led to the same festival being celebrated differently and having different legends attached to it! What is incredible about Indian social customs is that most of them are still practiced in much the same manner even to this day!

Women in Ancient India

Ancient India was quite liberal as far as women were concerned. They were well-educated and held in high respect. They also had the power to make decisions, especially for members of the household. Ancient Indian women had separate customs and rituals. Marriage rituals in particular were very unique. A custom known as *Swayamvara* allowed her to choose her husband from a group of men assembled at her father's house.

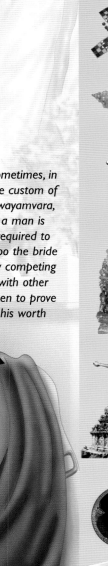

Sometimes, in the custom of Swayamvara, a man is required to woo the bride by competing with other men to prove his worth

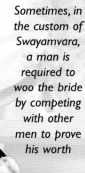

DID YOU KNOW?

Which is the festival of colours?

Holi or *Holika* is the festival of colours, celebrated since ancient times. Apart from singing and dancing, people smear each other with coloured water, powders and paint! This is done to celebrate the eternal love of Lord Krishna and his divine consort, Radhika.

Is any other legend attached to *Holi*?

Huge bonfires, lit on the eve of Holi, mark the ceremonial burning of the demoness, Holika. She was the sister of Hiranyakashyapu, a king of the *Asuras* or demons.

Was *Deepavali* an important festival in ancient India?

Deepavali is the festival celebrating the victory of good over evil. The stories behind it are many, but the message is the same. On this day, streets and homes are lit with lamps. People wear new clothes and burst firecrackers!

The people celebrate Holi, the festival of colours, with gay abandon

Rangoli continues to be an integral part of daily life in India

What is *Rangoli*?

It is a traditional art of decorating courtyards and doorsteps of houses and temples. Women drew complicated designs with rice flour and water. It was believed that decorating courtyards invited the deities and brought good luck!

Did ancient Indians believe in astrology?

Ancient Indians believed that a person's destiny depended on the position of the stars and planets at the time of birth. Traditionally, these details are meticulously recorded on a palm leaf scroll. This *janmapatri* or horoscope is first read out during a baby's *namkaranam* (naming ceremony) and is consulted throughout his life.

What is the significance of *Tulsi* worship?

According to ancient Indian beliefs, the bed where the Holy Basil or *Tulsi* is planted, becomes pure and holy. According to mythology, *Tulsi* kept Yama or the God of Death away. That is why it is considered sacred and is worshipped by Indians even today.

Indian women worship the sacred Tulsi in their courtyards even today

What is a *muhurtam*?

Before starting any ceremony, journey or new project, ancient Indians consulted a special calendar called the *panchanga*. This helped to calculate an auspicious time or *muhurtam* for beginning any venture. Even today, Indians seek the right *muhurtam* for important events!

FACT BOX

- *Namaskaram* or *Namaste* is the traditional Indian greeting. It is done by clasping the palms together and bowing the head a little. The term is a combination of "namasya" meaning "bow" and "te" meaning "to you".

- The *bindi* is a traditional red dot worn by married Indian women on their foreheads. In ancient times, an Aryan groom used to mark his bride's forehead with his blood as a sign of his protection and possession over her!

- *Raksha Bandhan* or *Rakhi* was a tradition observed by Aryan women. Before the men left for battle, the womenfolk tied a sacred thread on their men's wrists. This was supposed to protect the person and remind him of his family duties!

Today, in India, sisters tie decorated bracelets like this on the wrists of their brothers during Rakshabandhan

DID YOU KNOW?

Did ancient Indians have a traditional way of eating meals?

Ancient Indians sat cross legged on the floor and ate their meals off banana leaves or plates made from banyan leaves. Sitting cross legged was believed to help digestion. Water was sprinkled around the leaf and a little food kept outside it, as an offering to ancestors. This is still followed on special occasions.

A traditional meal served on a freshly cut banana leaf

Did ancient Indians worship snakes?

Snake worship was popular even during the Harappan civilisation. The *Naga* tribe started this ancient custom. Snakes are still considered holy in India. On *Nagapanchami*, the snake festival, Indian women pour milk into snake pits and offer them eggs!

What is *chudakarma*?

It is one of the 16 *samskaras* or purification ceremonies that have been followed in India since Vedic times. It was believed that the hair at birth was impure and had to be shaved off at a certain age.

What is special about *Buddha Poornima*?

Buddha Poornima is the most important Buddhist festival. It falls on a full moon day in the month of *Vaisakh* (April-May). Not only was Buddha born on this day, but he also attained enlightenment and *Nirvana* (release from the cycle of birth and death) on this very day!

Did the ancient Indians bury their dead?

Early Harappans buried the dead. But the Aryans cremated their dead – with the exception of infants. They believed that fire purified the soul of the dead. Elaborate funeral rites were performed to free the soul and send it to the next world.

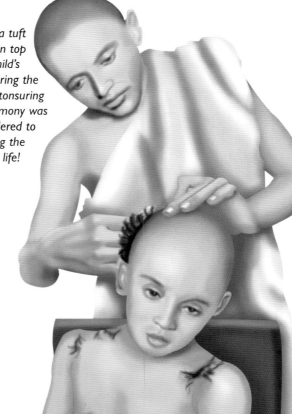

Leaving a tuft of hair on top of a child's head during the ritual tonsuring ceremony was considered to prolong the child's life!